Uncle Dan's Present

**Dan Ziatz and
Gloria Ziatz Sherman**

ISBN 978-1-0980-9993-0 (paperback)
ISBN 978-1-0980-9994-7 (digital)

Christian Faith Publishing, Inc.
832 Park Avenue
Meadville, PA 16335
www.christianfaithpublishing.com

Printed in the United States of America

This book is dedicated to my nieces, Tracy, Stephanie, Trish, Lori, and Maria, and to my nephews, Bobby, Craig, and David. It is also for my daughter, Natalie, and son, Stephen, who know most of what is here by heart, and for my granddaughters, Alyssa and Alana, and for all of God's children.

A merry heart does good like medicine.
—Proverbs 17:22 (NKJV)

I hope these pages are fun to read, encourage you, and honor God.

Thank you to my sister, Gloria Ziatz Sherman, who helped in putting this book together. It uses several literary devices, including one of my favorites—acronyms—to help us remember what is good, pleasing, and worthwhile. And thanks to my wonderful wife, Ruth Stanfield Ziatz, who is my Wonder Woman. She says some of my thoughts are corny, and I say, "Enjoy the corn."

Contents

Acronyms

An **acronym** is a word or a shortened version of a series of words, made up of the *first letter of each word in the series.*

Following are twenty-six acronyms, one for each letter of the alphabet. Some are really good, but some are only okay. Choose a few that you like best. **For those that are only okay,** *see if you can come up with something better.*

1. **ASAP—A**lways **S**ay **A P**rayer
    Some people think ASAP means "as soon as possible," but saying a prayer is better because it takes stress out of the situation.

2. **BIBLE**—**B**asic **I**nstructions **B**efore **L**eaving **E**arth
   The Bible reveals
   who God is,
   His love for you,
   what He likes,
   what He doesn't like,
   how to have a good life,
   what's happened in the past,
   and what's coming next.

3. **CARE**—**C**onsider **A**nd **R**espect **E**veryone

4. **DO**—**D**ivine **O**pportunities
   Open your eyes. They are all around you.

5. **EGO**—**E**dging **G**od **O**ut
   Focusing on self

6. **FAITH**—**F**or **A**ll **I** **T**rust **H**im

7. **GOSPEL**—**G**od's **O**nly **S**on **P**rovides **E**ternal **L**ife

8. **HOPE**—**H**is **O**ngoing **P**resence **E**mpowers

9.   **IT**—**I**nspired **T**alent
      Everyone has a gift from God, but not everyone has IT.
      You know IT when you see IT.

10.   **JESUS CHRIST**—**J**esus **E**ternally **S**aves **U**s **S**inners; **C**ertainly **H**is **R**esurrection **I**s **S**upreme **T**ruth

11.   **KINDNESS**—**K**eep **I**ncluding, **N**ever **D**isrespect—
      Notice, **E**ncourage, **S**erve, **S**upport

12.   **LOVE**—**L**ifting **O**ther **V**ictims **E**ternally
      We are all victims of sin, and we all need to be loved and lifted in prayer.

13.   **MERCY**—**M**erciful **E**ternal **R**edeemer **C**hooses **Y**ou
      Jesus chooses you, and you have a choice to make too.
      Joshua said, "*As for me and my family, we will serve the Lord*" (Joshua 24:15 NLT).

14.   **NOW**—**N**otice **O**pportunities **W**henever
      Be in the present. Wherever you are, *be all there.*

15. **OVER ALL—O**ne Victorious, **E**ternal, **R**eigning, **A**wesome, **L**oving Lord

16. **PEACE—P**erfect **E**ase **A**nd **C**ontented **E**njoyment

17. **QUIET—Q**uality, **U**ninterrupted, **I**nspirational, **E**ssential **T**ime

18. **REST—R**elaxed **E**njoyment, **S**erene **T**rust

19. **SUCCESS—S**howing **U**p **C**an **C**ause **E**xcellence **S**tep by **S**tep
    This is so important! **Just show up!**

20. **TRUST—T**otal **R**eliance **U**pon the **S**avior **T**oday
    Trust in Jesus.

21. **UNITE—U**nify **N**eighbors, **I**nitiate **T**houghtful **E**ncounters

22. **VALOR—V**aliant **A**ctions **L**ift **O**ur **R**edeemer
    Courage reflects the presence of God with us.

23. **Wisdom**—**W**ise **I**nstruction **S**treaming **D**own **O**n **M**ankind
"But the wisdom from above is first pure, then peace-loving, gentle, compliant, full of mercy and good fruits, unwavering, without pretense" (James 3:17 CSB).

24. **X Factor**—There is no **X** factor.
An X factor is an unknown. There is no X factor for God because God is omniscient (all-knowing).

25. **Yes**—**Y**our **E**ternal **S**alvation
Saying "Yes" to Jesus saves you from an eternity apart from God.

26. **Zeal**—**Z**estful **E**nergetic **A**ffirmative **L**iving

That concludes the alphabet, but following are some bonus acronyms just for fun. Find a favorite to memorize.

ATTITUDE—**A**pproach **T**esting **T**imes **I**n **T**rust **U**sing **D**ivine **E**mpowerment

FAMILY—**F**ather **A**nd **M**other, **I** **L**ove **Y**ou

FEAR—**F**rightening **E**xpectations **A**ppearing **R**eal

FROG—**F**ully **R**ely **O**n **G**od

GLORY—**G**od's **L**ove **O**ffer **R**eaches **Y**ou
It shines on you every day.

GRACE—**G**od's **R**iches **A**t **C**hrist's **E**xpense
You may have heard this acronym before, but it's so good!

KISS—**K**eep **I**t **S**hort and **S**imple
Or Short and Sweet.

LIVE—**L**ive **I**n **V**ital **E**xuberance

PLAN—**P**repare **L**asting **A**chievements **N**ow

SCRIPTURE—**S**urely **C**hrist's **R**eality **I**s **P**ure **T**ruth—**U**nveiled, **R**evealed, **E**xpressed

SHINE—**S**how **H**is **I**nfinite **N**oteworthy **E**nlightenment

SIN—**S**elfishness, **I**mpatience, **N**egligence

TELL—**T**ell **E**veryone **L**ive and **L**ove
Send flowers to people who are alive. Don't wait until they're dead.

TGIF—**T**hank **G**od **I**'m **F**orgiven
This is far more important than "Thank God It's Friday."

THINK—Ask yourself, "Is what I'm about to say **T**houghtful, **H**elpful, **I**nspiring, **N**ecessary, and **K**ind?"

WIN—**W**hat's **I**mportant **N**ow (Right now!)
To win at anything, you need to be in the present—not the past or the future but what's happening right now.
Be there, all there!

ZOOM—**Z**eal **O**vercomes **O**bstacles **M**ightily
Turn obstacles into opportunities.

Aphorisms

An ***aphorism*** is a short saying that expresses *wisdom or a general truth.* See if you can find wisdom in what follows.

- **Whether you think a glass is half-full or half-empty, you're right!**

- **Know God, know peace.**
  No God, no peace.

  Yesterday is history.
  Tomorrow is a mystery.
  Today is a gift.
  That's why we call it the present

- **Live every day as if it were your last day on earth. One day, you'll be right.**

If this were your last twenty-four hours, what would you do?

Life is mysterious. It makes no sense at all without God.

- **To get better, you have to lose.**
  To get better in sports, you have to compete with someone better than you, and that means you will lose. That's okay. That's how you get better. To be the best, you have to compete with the best.

- **Faith allows us to see beyond the visible to what is *true*.**

  > *Faith means knowing that some-thing is real even when we do not see it.* (Hebrews 11:1b ICB)

  If you don't have faith, talk to God about it. A man once brought his son to Jesus, not sure that Jesus could heal the boy. He said to Jesus,

  > *I do believe; help me overcome my unbelief!* (Mark 9:24b NLT)

The Bible says,

> Anyone who comes to Him
> must believe that He exists
> and that He rewards those who
> earnestly seek Him. (Hebrews
> 11:6b NIV)

- **What we think and say and do**
  Shows our attitude through and through.
  We honor God or we sin in three ways: TWA
  In our **T**houghts, **W**ords, and **A**ctions.

- **Courage is as courage does.**
  "Success is not final, failure is not fatal: it is the
  courage to continue that counts."—Winston
  Churchill

  > *Haven't I commanded you: be*
  > *strong and courageous? Do not*
  > *be afraid or discouraged, for the*
  > *Lord your God is with you wher-*
  > *ever you go.* (Joshua 1:9 CSB)

- **How you perceive a situation is more powerful than the situation itself.**

  Challenge or Pressure? Suppose you are in the last five seconds of a basketball game, and your team is down by one point. You get fouled and go to the free throw line. You think, *Oh no, what if I let the team down?* You are under pressure.

  But if you think, *Lord, I've practiced this shot thousands of times. Give me the ball. I'm ready for this!* You are up to the challenge!

- **We can't encourage people too much.**

  Look for what is right, not what is wrong. Tell people when they've done something right.

- **There is a Christian bar of soap.**

  > *"If we confess our sins, He is faithful and just to forgive us our sins and to cleanse us from all unrighteousness"* (1 John 1:9 NIV).

To confess means we agree with God that we have sinned.

The Bible says, "*All have sinned, and come short of the glory of God*" (Romans 3:23 NIV).

- **Fear of the Lord is a good fear.**

  Fear of the Lord is an awareness of the awesome, holy, just, and almighty God. The Spirit who will keep us accountable in all of our thoughts, words, and actions.

- **Go for the best.**

  Good, better, best—
  Never let it rest
  Until good is better,
  And better is best.

- **Remember to keep the main thing the main thing, and there is only one main thing.**

- **There will always be prayer in schools as long as teachers give tests.**

- **Integrity means to know right and to do right.**

The Bible teaches us what is right.
Solomon prayed that God would give him wisdom so that he could rule God's people well.

> *Give me an understanding mind so that I can govern your people well and know the difference between what is right and what is wrong. For who by himself is able to carry such a heavy responsibility?* (1 Kings 3:9 TLB)

- **Lift it up—give it to God.**
  If you know how to worry, you know how to focus your thoughts.
  The next step is to lift them up, let go, and let God.

- **Be a prayer warrior, not a prayer worrier.**
  Prayer is positive. Worry is negative.

> *Don't worry about anything, but in everything, through prayer and petition with thanksgiving, present your requests to God. And*

> *the peace of God, which surpasses all understanding, will guard your hearts and minds in Christ Jesus.* (Philippians 4:6–7 CSB)

- **LOVE is the greatest motivating force in the world.**
  Love always seeks the best for the one who is loved. It was because of love that God sent His Son. It was because of love that Jesus went to the cross.

> *For God loved the world in this way: He gave his one and only Son, so that everyone who believes in him will not perish but have eternal life.* (John 3:16 CSB)

Vowels for Success

A—Attitude
E—Effort
I—Improvement
O—Opportunities
U—Understanding

Vowels for Failure

A—Annoying
E—Exasperating
I—Irritating
O—Obnoxious
U—Ungrateful

Uncle Dan's Recommended Activities

- Start your day with God's Word.
- Take five minutes a day to read a devotional together with your family.
- Encourage—Pour courage into people. We can't do this too much.
- Take online Bible quizzes. Challenge yourself.

Attitude

Your attitude determines how you see everything and how pleasant or unpleasant your life will be. The best part is that you can change your attitude.

> "Folks are usually about as happy as
> they make their minds up to be."
> —Abraham Lincoln

Uncle Dan's M&Ms for attitude
- **M**indset
- **M**ental State
- **M**ood

Before a person can learn **what** a good attitude is, he first needs to know *who* demonstrated the best attitude.

Jesus lived out the best attitude and demonstrated it on the cross. He prayed for those who crucified Him, asking God to forgive them. This is our greatest example of love. He prayed for His enemies while they were killing him.

> *No one has greater love than this: to lay down his life for his friends.* (John 15:13 CSB)

> Jesus said, *"But I say to you who listen, 'love your enemies, do what is good to those who hate you, bless those who curse you, and pray for those who mistreat you"* (Luke 6:27–28 CSB).

New Be Attitudes

With the help of the Holy Spirit, a good attitude can be developed.

> *But the fruit of the Spirit is love, joy, peace, patience, kindness, goodness, faithfulness, gentleness, and self-control. The law is not against such things. (Galatians 5:22–23 CSB)*

LOVE is the attitude you can *choose*
    when you encounter the *unlovable.*
JOY is the attitude you can *choose*
    when you encounter *problems in life.*
PEACE is the attitude you can *choose*
    when you encounter *conflict.*
PATIENCE is the attitude you can *choose*
    when you encounter *suffering.*
KINDNESS is the attitude you can *choose*
    when you encounter *unkindness.*
GOODNESS is the attitude you can *choose*
    when you encounter *evil.*
GENTLENESS is the attitude you can *choose*
    when you encounter *harsh treatment.*

FAITHFULNESS is the attitude you can *choose*
when you encounter *unfaithfulness.*
SELF-CONTROL is the attitude you can *choose*
when people and situations are out of control.

Attitude Acrostic

An **acrostic** is writing in which the first letter of a line or section begins with a letter that spells a word.

Awareness can improve your attitude.
Awareness starts by observing what others do.
Learn from the good,
Reject the bad.
A good attitude
will make you glad.

Think and rethink to improve your attitude
What should you think about? Think about good things!

> *Finally, brothers and sisters, whatever is true, whatever is honorable, whatever is right, whatever is pure, whatever is lovely, whatever is commendable, if there is any excellence and if anything worthy of praise, think about these things.* (Philippians 4:8 NASB)

Try, try again.

Be persistent. Just as *The Little Engine That Could* said, "I think I can, I think I can," and kept trying and finally made it, so should we try, try again, knowing that we can never fail if we never ever quit. And regarding persistence, the Bible says,

> *Never stop praying.*
> (1 Thessalonians 5:17 NLT)

> *One day Jesus told his disciples a story to show that they should always pray and never give up. "There was a judge in a certain city," he said, "who neither feared God nor cared about people. A widow of that city came to him repeatedly, saying, 'Give me justice in this dispute with my enemy.' The judge ignored her for a while, but finally he said to himself, 'I don't fear God or care about people, but this woman is driving me crazy. I'm going to see that she gets justice, because she is*

*wearing me out with her constant
requests!'"* (Luke 18:1–5 NLT)

Include others. This is essential for a good attitude.

Jesus included everyone. He included the rich, poor, healthy, blind, deaf, lame, crippled, tax collectors, and others. Just as you like to be included, include others by following the golden rule.

*Do to others as you would like them
to do to you.* (Luke 6:31 NLT)

Thank God and others.

An attitude of gratitude is what we need if we want to win in life. It is the key to success. We often take our family and our health for granted. Both are fragile and far more important than wealth. Learn to appreciate and enjoy what you have.

On one occasion, Jesus cured ten lepers, and sadly only one returned to thank Him. Here's the story—

*As Jesus continued on toward
Jerusalem, he reached the border
between Galilee and Samaria.*

As he entered a village there, ten men with leprosy stood at a distance, crying out, "Jesus, Master, have mercy on us!"

He looked at them and said, "Go show yourselves to the priests." And as they went, they were cleansed of their leprosy.

One of them, when he saw that he was healed, came back to Jesus, shouting, "Praise God!" He fell to the ground at Jesus' feet, thanking him for what he had done. This man was a Samaritan.

Jesus asked, "Didn't I heal ten men? Where are the other nine? Has no one returned to give glory to God except this foreigner?" (Luke 17:11–18 NLT)

Use the gifts and abilities God has given you. God has given each person at least one special gift to be used for others.

- If you see someone without a smile, give them one of yours.

- If you have a good smile, smile people in and smile people out, like a greeter at church.
- If you are a teacher, teach well.
- If you are a baker, bake an apple pie and give a piece to Uncle Dan.
- Whatever you do, do it for the glory of God.

> *Work willingly at whatever you do, as though you were working for the Lord rather than for people.* (Colossians 3:23 NLT)

Develop improved self-talk.

Some people think in negative terms, which doesn't bring out their best. They say, "I can't do this," or "I can't do that," or "I always do poorly on tests." Instead say, **"Lord, I'll do my best and let you do the rest."** Then do your best. He will do the rest!

In baseball, if you hit over .300, you are considered very good, but think about it—seven out of ten times at bat, you'll be out. Don't expect perfection. No one was perfect except Jesus.

Enthuse

The word *enthuse* comes from the Greek word *enthuiasmos*, which means to have God in you, the breath of life. It is related to divine energy.

God gives you the ability to be energetic.

Be zealous. Have zeal appeal.

Enthusiasm is an attitude that is contagious and worth catching.

MORE ABOUT ATTITUDE

If I say to you, **"'Tude Dude,"** that is a compliment. It means you have a great attitude. It means you are **rethinking thinking,** not just reacting.

> *Your attitude should be the kind that was shown us by Jesus Christ.* (Philippians 2:6 NLT)

On the other hand, if I say to you **"Wimp City,"** that means you need to check your attitude. It means you have **stinking thinking**.

Scott Hamilton, a retired American figure skater and Olympic gold medalist who had three brain tumors and spent four years in and out (mostly in) of children's hospitals, said, "The only disability in life is a bad attitude."

If you encounter a jerk (someone with a bad attitude), say, "God loves you, and I'm trying."

Remember, you may be a jerk yourself at times. Also remember,

Jesus loves you,

God loves you,

Uncle Dan loves you, and don't you forget it!

And always remember that,

> *Nothing can ever separate us from God's love. Death can't, and life can't. The angels can't, and the demons can't. Our fears for today, our worries about tomorrow, and even the powers of hell can't keep God's love away. Nothing in all creation will ever be able to separate us from the love of God that is revealed in Christ Jesus our Lord.* (Romans 8:38–39 NLT)

About the Authors

Dan Ziatz received a bachelor of arts degree from William Jewell College, a master of arts degree from Western Illinois University, and a PhD from the University of Utah. He taught and coached football, wrestling, and track and field at the high school and college level for nine years and subsequently taught in the College of Physical Activity and Sport Sciences at West Virginia University from 1973 to 2014, when he retired.

Dr. Ziatz was the coordinator of the first principles of coaching online courses for Special Olympics in the country. He is a long-time member of the board of directors for the Fellowship of Christian Athletes at West Virginia University, the author of ten publications, including two scientific publications, and the recipient of grants from the W. K. Kellogg Community Partnership and the WVU Foundation. He is a father of two children and two grandchildren.

Gloria Ziatz Sherman received a bachelor of arts degree from Florida State University, a master of arts degree and a master of science degree from Central Washington University. She taught English at Central Washington University from 1976–1984, as a graduate assistant and adjunct faculty member. She wrote and edited newsletters and held administrative positions at the Boeing Company from 1984–2006. She has participated in short-term missions in Hong Kong, South Africa, and Thailand, and has 5 children, 5 stepchildren, 13 grandchildren, and 5 great-grandchildren.

Art and Gloria Sherman, Ruth and Dan Ziatz